JAMES STEVENSON
Quick! Turn the Page!

Greenwillow Books New York

Watercolor paints and a black pen
were used for the full-color art.
The text type is Bryn Mawr
Book and Bold.
Copyright © 1990 by
James Stevenson
All rights reserved.
No part of this book
may be reproduced or
utilized in any form
or by any means.
electronic or mechanical.
including photocopying.
recording. or by any
information storage and
retrieval system.
without permission in writing
from the Publisher.
Greenwillow Books.
a division of William
Morrow & Company. Inc..
105 Madison Avenue.
New York. NY 10016.

Printed in Hong Kong by
South China Printing Company (1988) Ltd.
First Edition
10 9 8 7 6 5 4 3 2 1

Library of Congress
Cataloging-in-Publication Data

Stevenson. James (date)
Quick! turn the page! / James Stevenson.
p.   cm.
Summary: The reader is encouraged
to turn the page and view
the amusing results.
ISBN 0-688-09308-6.
ISBN 0-688-09309-4 (lib. bdg.)
1.Literary recreations.
[1. Literary recreations.]
I. Title.
PZ7.S84748Qu   1990
[E]—dc20
89-34616 CIP AC

Sarah is sick of winter.

Quick! Turn the page!

Eddie has nobody to play with. *Quick! Turn the page!*

The birds are sleeping.

Turn the page quietly . . .

Too loud!

Lance, the turtle, is tired. *Quick! Turn the page!*

How many Easter eggs can an Easter Bunny juggle?

Turn the page.

Quite a lot.

But how does he get them down?

Turn the page again.

Friends help.

TWO PLUS TWO EQUALS...

When Emily does her homework,
nothing disturbs her.

Quick! Turn the page!

Turn the page again.

...FOUR.

Ralph is trying a new diet food.

Quick! Turn the page!

It works!

Arthur's room is a total mess.   Quick! Turn the page!

Herbert the mouse wants to get to the other room.

Turn the page.

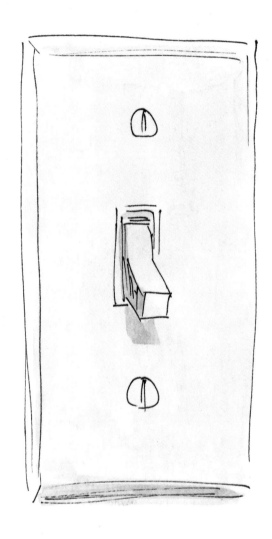

Would you please turn the light off?

Dark, isn't it?

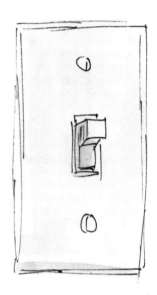

Would you
turn
the light
back on?

*Now turn
the page.*

The monster wants something to eat.

Quick! Turn the page!

Here comes a snowball...

Quick! Turn the page!

Too late.

This time... *don't turn the page!*

THE END

(Told you not to turn the page!)